From Elsewhere

FROM ELSEWHERE

Ciaran Carson

WAKE FOREST UNIVERSITY PRESS

First North American edition

ISBN 978-1-930630-70-3

Library of Congress Catalog Number 2014922078

Designed and typeset in ITC Galliard CC
by Nathan W. Moehlmann,
Goosepen Studio & Press

From Elsewhere was first published by The Gallery Press
in Ireland in 2014 and edited by Peter Fallon.

Wake Forest University Press
WFUPRESS.WFU.EDU
Post Office Box 7333
Winston-Salem, NC 27109

for my students

Contents

APROPOS

PART ONE

PART TWO

PART THREE

Apropos

L'autre: The Other

This book consists of translations from the French poet Jean Follain, faced by 'original' poems inspired by those translations: spins or takes on them in other words. Translations of the translations as it were.

I came upon Follain by chance. Some time ago, while working on translating some of the prose poems of Francis Ponge into verse, I discovered that Ponge was a friend of Follain, whom I'd never heard of until then. When I looked him up on the internet one of the first things I found was a version of the first poem in this present book, '*Soulier renoué*: Shoelace Tied'. Such a humble poem, yet how resonant, how mysterious. I was immediately taken by it, and proceeded to immerse myself in Follain's work.

When one translates one cannot avoid taking liberties of one kind or another; and perhaps one takes a special liberty in translating Follain, whose attachment to his native language was such that he declared himself unable to learn any other. At the age of sixteen he was sent to Leeds to learn English, and spent much of his time in his boarding-house reading whatever French newspapers he could find to console himself in his exile. *Le mot fait corps avec la chose*, he said, the word makes body with the thing, or the word embodies the thing, as one might say in English; and no other word but the French would do him. The only word for 'bread' was *le pain*; his friend, the Breton poet Guillevic, recounts how Follain, with a playful glint in his eye, would insist that no other word could possibly exist for such a thing, and in a manner of speaking he is of course correct, since French bread is another matter to English bread. *Le pain* belongs to a system of very different semantic weights, textures and measures; like wine, or rather *le vin*, it is rooted in the culture of France, in its linguistic *terroir*. It is often said that translation is impossible; yet it is done, and needs to be done. It has also been said that poetry itself is a kind of translation.

I'm not sure at what point it occurred to me

to double the book. Perhaps it has something to do with the format of my book *For All We Know* (2008), which is divided into two parts, with the titles of the poems in Part Two repeating the titles of the poems in Part One, in the same order, each of the titles thus being revisited from a different point of view. I do know that the word 'fetch', which is used in several contexts in that book, was in my mind throughout the writing of *From Elsewhere*. It is a word that has long fascinated me, and many of the definitions in the lengthy entry in the Oxford English Dictionary seem relevant to what I thought I might be doing. A fetch is the act of fetching, bringing from a distance, or reaching after: it is something brought from elsewhere, an act of translation in other words. To fetch is to draw or 'borrow' from a source. It is to derive etymologically. It is to go in quest of. In sailing, it is an act of tacking, and also to get into the wake of a vessel, as I fetched myself into the wake of Follain, and hence fetched my course, like a sailor who after a long fetch at sea comes home with a far-fetched tale. A fetch is the apparition, double, or wraith of a living person. A shadowy counterpart, as my poems might be to those of Follain.

Follain very rarely uses the first person in his poetry, yet we cannot doubt the personal experience that lies behind many of the poems. Guillevic remarks that if Rimbaud said *Je est un autre* (I is another), then in Follain — *chez Follain*, as the French has it — the 'other' is indispensable in discovering the 'I'. So I find myself in the other of Follain, questing and fetching the poems from another language, from the elsewhere of his territory.

Jean Follain was born in the home of his paternal grandmother in the village of Canisy in Normandy in 1903. His father was a teacher in the nearby city of Saint-Lô, and Follain attended school there, spending the holidays in Canisy, the inspiration for many of his poems. He was aged eleven when war broke out in 1914, and says that had he been born just a year later his poetry would not have been that which it was, a memorial to a lost world. And when he came to view Saint-Lô in the aftermath of its almost complete destruction by Allied bombing in 1944, he declared that the power of things to endure had been effectively annihilated; yet they abided in the memory, and through poetry might exist in an eternal present.

In 1921 he went to study law at the University of Caen, and in 1927 was admitted to the bar in Paris. During the Second World War he adopted a passive neutrality, while discreetly supporting those writers who opposed the Vichy regime. He immersed himself in writing. His prose memoir *Canisy* was published in 1942, his book of poems *Usage du temps* in 1943. In 1951 he left the bar to practise as a magistrate in Charleville, the home town of Rimbaud. Still resident in Paris in the rambling apartment in Place des Vosges which he shared with his wife, the painter Madeleine Dinès, he would commute to Charleville by train.

Follain was devoted to ceremony and ritual to an almost sacramental degree. Noncommittal in his religious beliefs, he was nevertheless fascinated by the offices and rubrics of the Roman Catholic church, and was known to have rebuked several priests, including the celebrant of the Christmas Day Mass in Notre Dame, and the archbishop of Rouen, for neglecting to wear the correct vestments for the liturgy. He liked to ponder such questions as the consequences of an insect happening to fall into the chalice at the moment of transubstantiation, or the accidental vomiting of the sacred host. He was a member of several dinner clubs associated with the arts, the legal profession and the wider world of politics, where he was known for the wit and erudition of his table talk. Gourmand or gourmet according to circumstance, he extolled the virtues of the peasant cooking of his childhood, and wrote a treatise on the potato, *Célebration de la pomme de terre*, published in a little volume some fifteen centimetres square, appropriately bound in sackcloth. He was invariably properly dressed for every occasion.

The last entry in his diary, dated 9th March 1971, reads '*Dîner Vieux-Papier*'. *Le Vieux Papier* is an association devoted to the study of paper ephemera such as menus, playing cards, railway tickets, cheese labels, school exercise books, holy pictures, wine labels, theatre programmes, greeting cards, board games, diaries and the like. Returning home from the dinner shortly after midnight on the 10th, Jean Follain was knocked down and killed by a car on Place de la Concorde. His book *Espaces d'instants* was in press at the time and was published a few days later. He was a firm believer that poems, after being written, should be *mise en cave*, that is, laid down like wine in the cellar, and sampled in due course to see if they were up to the mark. Hence a good many of his books have been fetched from the cellar and published posthumously, having passed the test of time.

Il vit, il voit le temps comme
des fractions de l'éternité.
— Guillevic, 1993

He saw, he sees time as fractions of eternity.

CIARAN CARSON,
Belfast, August 2014

Part One

Soulier renoué: Shoelace Tied

When evening waves
its bank of clouds
one sees the grass fires
raise their smoke
flowers grow in the sunken lanes
there's still a glimpse of daylight
and a boy in an iron-grey smock
bows to a rut
to tie his shoelace
no slack in his life
no trace of absence.

Out

Thinking
the end of the world to be
at the horizon the boy walked
for hours; after his people
scoured the fields for miles around
crying his name
to the four winds
to no reply
at twilight they found him
where he'd last been seen
standing in the stable yard
unable to say anything
about where he had been
in that full circle he had walked
beyond 'out'
having no words
for what he had seen
beyond those that were of home.

Sans le langage: Without Language

The sadness of voice without language
under a sky of racing clouds
wearies the body
going on endlessly
talking every which where
when noises have made their silences
and substance languishes.
Bunches of keys in their pockets
those that live with death
return home.

In Memory

As he told it
when the boy
he was stumbled
on the well
in the derelict brickyard
deep as a brick mill chimney
leaning over the rim
he shouted
the two syllables
of his name
deep down into it
to hear his echo.
Now that the man
he would become
is dead
that unfathomable
darkness
echoes
still.

L'île brûlée: The Burnt Island

Concerning the burnt island
there is a long memory
of all the shadows of inhabitants
and those of ploughs and harrows.
On a certain morning a great noise
was made and shook all the rooms.
Reality dwells
in a child's hand, writing with such force
on the ruled paper
that by the second line he pierced it through
and made the steel nib bend
then an icy wind arose
which made the naked branches bend.

Timing Device

As with thunder
the rumble comes
after the flash the shimmer
of a tolled bell stroke
after stroke reverberating
heard one certain day
but now but a glimmer
of all such memories of bells
a newsreel flicker
the skeleton of a building
or its scaffolding
he cannot remember
the number of victims
let alone their names
or in what month of what year
that certain day fell.

Le calme: The Calm

The image on the wall
shows God emerging from the clouds.
The sound of a pen
in this long narrow
country office
echoes from afar
after the wars.
The mud of the marshes beyond
barely stirs
a hand advances
to seize a rabbit
which will die there and then.
From a tree in full leaf
a squirrel hears the cries
and does not understand the broken calm.

The Word

If according to the proverb
God sees the black insect
passing on the black stone
how much more does He see
that boy's hand stealing forth
to pluck the apple
from the apple-box
or the red insect falling
into the chalice to commune
with the communion wine
at the moment of its being
turned into blood by the uttering of a word.

La guenille: The Rag

Powerless
to imitate the bird
the rag hangs from the branch
red beside the sweet apple
the bird flown the apple fallen
it stays where it is
flaunting the chill of ages
and its colour in the silence;
men are organizing
in the dark times
not far from this tatter marking
nothing but the space it occupies.

Sunset

The street lamps come on
one by one
as an armoured car speeds
into the oncoming dark
the north wind picks up
from lamp post
after lamp post
along the stretch of demarcated road
the union
flags begin to flicker in their tatters.

Des fleurs: Concerning Flowers

Flowers seem to watch
gathered in great number
at the edges of a gorge
and one could well fear these clumps
unsleeping
in their enclaves of leaf-mould,
no miller no tumbril
but the solitary sky
of a province
where sometimes a great bowl breaks
among its painted flowers.

Reverberation

From time to time
following the rumble of thunder
or a bomb
upon a mantelpiece
a Dresden vase crowded
with open-mouthed flowers
trembles about
to topple
over.

L'aube: The Dawn

A rooftop then the star
paling above
caught the eye of a man
who felt himself taken back
to the endgame of a legal process
the signs below
unveiled their words of gold,
wood, iron, stone
imposed their presence
a wide open window
showed an ochre wall and a cupboard
and a hand placing an iron spoon
on an earthenware dish
where it was chipped ages ago.

Twilight

A painted brickwork
sign fading
high on the gable wall
he took one word to be
pharmacy, another perhaps
a person's name
the letters blurred
by glimpses of brick
dawning back
from ages ago
the sky above the gable
he imagined thundery
under it
bottles of cobalt blue
ads for razor blades
next door the black
glass of the undertaker's
window.

Page franchie: A Page Ventured

In an office on a day of routine gloom
a sheet of paper
beside a gutted loaf imbibes black ink
within the resonating hour
a minuscule insect utterly alive
vibrates, ventures forth reddish-brown
across the written page.

The Blotting-paper

He opened a book
he hadn't opened for years
a sheet of blotting-paper fell
from between its leaves
it looked like the map of a city
whose streets petered out into blank
or led into blot
overwritten with false beginnings
and no real endings;
and he tried to remember the hour
he first had lost himself
in that labyrinth of words once almost
decipherable by
the mirror in the dim hallway
of a house no longer
on the map.

Le poignard: The Dagger

An old traitor's dagger
from a melodrama
was discovered by a gloved hand
plucking nettles.
The silence was vast and powerful
as in childhood
fields of apple trees
village flowers
narrow gates
composed themselves into a long evening
the colour of the absolute
bathed the countryside where
pollen from a fleur-de-lis
had fallen on
the dagger-blade.

Under the Apple Tree

The war being over
so they say
years ago
he turned his hand
to writing of the past
before the war
the child he was reached
for a cup on a high shelf
afterwards remembering
the dimples and bobbles
of its painted blossoms
before it fell,
the man remembers as he stumbles
in a garden among the nettles
on a typewriter
turning to rust
beside a broken cup.

Le chasseur: The Hunter

Someone day after day dreams
of hunting in a world without end
the game that haunts
land and water
as far as utter darkness
and that all doors remain open.
Off goes this man
to hunch under cover
before crossroad after crossroad.
Moribund one, his wife says to him
think no more on these violent deaths
in the depths of the woods.

Wake

Night after night the couple
turn in their bed
talking or turning towards
and then away from
the murmur of a far-off helicopter
over trouble somewhere,
speak of whose turn
might be next
and whether they
who speak will be
upon this earth
to look on yet
another face
shimmering in the candlelight
of the afterlife
blank.

Des pas secrets: Secret Steps

She hears steps
never quite reaching her
a faint voice says to her
don't count on a miracle
still she hears whatever it is
moving away to the end of the corridor
that which sets her atremble
on the plain of fog prolongs itself
into the course of human hours.

Phantom Call

The apparatus resonates
he picks up
handset from cradle
puts earphone to ear
and mouthpiece to mouth
speaks
listens for the other
to realize
he is
the man at the other end
of nothing.

La clef: The Key

The dark key attached
to the heavy copper ring
with a day number
in the white night
that hangs from a nail in the vast inn
has been taken by the sleeper
who now from the wood of the bed lets go
a hand gloved in mud.

The Beyond

That windows too may have locks
but only on the inside
lest the window be a door
once more occurred to him
he climbed out into the night
to go where he had gone
before to wake up
at dawn in his own bed
clad in mud
from the neck down
remembering nothing beyond
unlocking the window.

Un soir se refait: Reprise

An evening recoups its losses
in the shuddering of wheatfields
hammerings on doors
armoires emptied
getting up from its knees
from under the hems
of the black robe
flecked with sunlight
a beast slouches to its corner
untroubled by the days of horror
which reprise a couple
at the turning of a road
swamped with birds.

The Odds

A burst of gunfire
in the bookmaker's shop
where men are smoking
watching the horses
on television
one of them dying
as the pigeons
on the square outside
transform themselves
into a purple cloud boiling up
from the cobblestones
to the sound of their own applause.

Dans les temps: When

In the days of the interminable retinues
of the Sun King
it went below freezing
one night on this piece of earth
the man after drinking
wiped his blond moustache
the woman barely noticed
the crystals of frost
the future centuries a long army
lay in wait
upon the mountain peaks.

Before the War

No corridor
but room after interconnecting room
leads to the royal chamber
behind locked doors
a fire near to
expiry
the windows frosted from within
the king's breath
as he breathes and sleeps
alone slowly turning
his beard
hoary.

L'affiche: The Poster

The boy bouncing a barrel hoop along
for want of a toy one
runs whooping to himself
but to him who comes to spell out
under the N and the imperial eagle
the words of the conscription poster
the old man in the uneasy sunshine
drinking a glass of rough cider
has only this to say:
'the next century will be worse'
in spite of which the lovers pass him by
singing as they go.

Urban Warfare

A soldier from
a foot patrol
hunkers in a doorway gun scanning
the length of the street whatever might happen next
unblinkingly
a woman passes
wheeling a pram,
the soldier remembers
a child opening his eyes
to a blue sky a white cloud
the sound of a bird
singing from a rooftop.

Contours: Contours

From time to time the harness maker
would turn his hand
to barbering armed with razor
everything stayed coiled
within him and about him
his great forked beard
his horse collars
and the loops of Brandenburg braid
on the hussar's dolman,
his son who stayed where he was
on a broken threshold
primed and ready
for other times.

Closed Circuit

He is the regular whose eye you avoid
because the only time you did not
yours were met with a blank
still you think he knows
who you might be,
drinking under the TV
that shows the grey
of who's outside
finger on the buzzer,
and if he does not then
you do not know this man
who takes his gun apart
and reassembles it
three times a day
every day that passes
loads it
aims it.

Entailles: Furrows

A furrowed school table
reveals initials
roads get into a muddle
around the granite building
a Great Dane barks
in the shadows vegetation withers
someone says:
I am old
his hand bears the same veins
as in childhood
loaded with goods a ship leaves
the city to its rubble.

Mill Street

Alone in the dayroom
he would listen for
the murmur of the stream
that ran below the school
to be lost in the thrum
of the spinning mill
no longer there the one
he stares at on
a map of then
tall in his memory
above the wire-grilled windows
the courses of brick
go up and up
the teetering
height of the mill chimney
leading nowhere.

Signes: Signs

Sometimes when a customer in a drab restaurant
is shelling an almond
a hand happens to fall on his thin shoulder
he thinks twice about finishing his wine
the distant forest lies under snow
the sturdy servant girl has gone pale
she'd do well to forget the winter night
has she not often seen
on the last page
of a not too difficult book
the end word printed
in ornate capital letters?

The Appearance

There were letters missing
from the shop sign
in any case he couldn't see
what remained of the name
in his mind's eye
a bell tinkled
dwindling
into the wake of what
had gone before
he opened the door into
the indefinable gleam
of things biding their time
a glimmer of what had been
that he had just wandered
into there and then
with no memory
of where he had been.

Oeuvres: Men at Work

The eye is stopped
short by the furrows
made by a body
a tree rustles
under a sky like that
which covers Herculaneum.
Alongside the ruts
the seeker of vipers
thinks of his dead friend.
Hours later men
carrying thornproof sacks
set about setting up
a night of love.

Digging

Following the furrows
he came to a garden
festooned in gloomy hemlock
breathing its odour of mouse
the track still visible
leading to a shed built of old doors
one of which squeaked
open when pushed
to a smell of musty sackcloth,
and leaning in the dark a spade
betrayed
by its bright steel.

Ville haute: High City

By night garments are constructed
by indomitable women
with lively voices
to the smell of flesh in vogue
amidst the rubble.
By day once more
railings, pillars, turrets,
yellow tiles and ruptured walls
will be seen again
in the clear light of a city
piled on a high rock
for the edification of travellers.

Window

He bent to his task
at the keyboard as if about
to play an aria of which
the notes or words
were not yet known.
He stared at the blank
beyond the window
and began to touch-type
thinking of what had been
before the bomb
and typed some more.
He looked at the words
on screen and struck
the keys for print
the printer ticked
and ticked and then
disgorged a page
with nothing on it.

Croisées des routes: Paths Crossing

The white sun in the gardens
warms the invalids
a high thick hedge
conceals the gunshot ward
at the gates there's talk
of the price of wheat
he passes men carrying tools
stray hens
plumes covered in dust
schoolboys with dark scabs
on their scratches
opening their eyes so they might see
everything
under the burning cloudless blue.

Identity Parade

From the hospital ward
that overlooks a prison yard
the gunshot victim
watches them exercising
day after day
wondering if any
of the faces he sees now
are those he could not see
then hooded as they were
sometimes
one or other of them
seems to look up
to meet his eye
before he looks away.

Le présent: The Now

The tatters of a scarecrow
flap in the wind
that sweeps the terrain
a wall topped with broken bottles
is falling to bits
slender lizards
do not die there
nor do the children hell-bent
on firing stones at the sky
like lightning then
the Now shimmers
and flashes as it did when
empty of men.

Then

Fallen from some
unknown tree
the leaf stuck
to the mushroom
trembles
in a moonlit glade
a horseman passes by
vanishes
into the gloom.

Aux temps sombres: The Dark Times

Covert copse
and cottage
also flourish in the dark times
when men tremble
to hear the knock on the door;
on their bodies women
who carry messages
hear their dresses flutter
displace their shadows
with a fevered impulse
to exist in the light.

Remains

Given not so much as
a knock on the door
men disappear
no word for years
a mechanical digger
strips the ground,
men with spades move in.
A mother watches from the margin
envisioning a body
transfigured from the mire.

La constance: What Remains

Garments are shed one by one
in total peace a body is undressed
outside the houses
lights come on in byres
the night-workers
sleep on
a woman will have a dream
without an outcome
a man with the face of a child
will push a handcart
full of footmen's livery
relieved of its gold braid.

Revolution

The same tumbril
that, tilted, would dump
windfallen apples
into the cider press
now rumbles over
the red cobbles
of the market square
with its load of prisoners
ripe for the guillotine.

La recherche: The Hunt

The stemmed glass breaks
in this vulnerable day
full of clutter and jumble
and not in so many words
under a dark wardrobe
a girl hunts for a slipper
her supple body
can be heard breathing
in faded and lightly darned garments
sometimes the whole house trembles
founded as it is
on the brink of an abyss.

Covert

In the middle of the night
comes the clattering of the typewriter
spattering the page with words
the whole house shuddering
under the onslaught
the Dresden milkmaid figurine
falls from the mantelpiece
and shatters on the hearth
the fox in the back yard
scatters the mop and bucket
and runs for cover
under the trembling
stars echoing
far off
gunfire.

Le globe: The Globe

A village schoolboy took it upon himself
to bear to the village schoolmaster
a globe of the world
holding it aloft by its bronze pedestal
and the fire of the forge
illuminated the sphere and the wine sinking
down the gullets of the blacksmiths
in their dogskin aprons.

The Geography Lesson

Walking home from school
where he has been
drawing and colouring in
a map of Ireland
he takes an unwonted turn
into a street
where he has never been he sees
the painted kerbstones
bordering a waste ground
where the skeleton
of a child's perambulator smoulders
at the heart of a dead bonfire.

Félicité: Bliss

The least crack
in a windowpane or in a bowl
can lead back to the sheer bliss
of a splendid memory
things stripped
to show themselves fishbone-fine
sparkling in a stroke
of sunlight
but lost in the night
gorge themselves as well on the hours
be they long
or short.

Childhood

The merest flicker
of a flower stem is bent
by the water in
a glass vase at
the corner of the eye
refracted as it strikes
the mind as seen
before recurrently
as to when
or where it was
first glimpsed or gazed upon,
the corresponding flower
sometimes hovers over one
in memory if not dream
a perfume that is
nameless as is
the flower for now.

Part Two

Vie: Life

He is born a child
into a boundless landscape
half a century on
he is but a dead soldier
and it was there that this man
was seen to appear
and set down
a sack loaded with apples
two or three of which rolled out
a sound among those of a world
where a bird sang
on the stone slab of the threshold.

To Dream

Under a muttering of thunder
or the memory of a bomb
come from afar
this man tilts
the full of a tumbril
of windfalls
into the cellar bin
he has come to
in the dark to hear
a rumbling sound
of load on load
coming in to trouble
someone else's sleep,
whoever that man be
that came to dream him.

A l'écoute: Receiver

The vision lingers
trembling the hand which writes it down
in a room of the inn by starlight
evening drowns
the potato field.
When the farmer hears a footfall on the road
he leaves off digging
then turns on
his private listening
to the sounds of his world.

All Clear

Every ear tunes to the radio
to hear Westminster
toll, a voice giving out
by night
through the blackout searchlights crisscross
by dawn
it is all clear, the ruins silent
save for
the footfall of a drunken soldier
the echo of his song.

L'embellie: Clear Spell

The roofs of a bleak village
stagnate ever greener
under a sullen zenith
when in a sudden clear spell
a ray of fidelity
lights on a murderous face;
long hair streaming over the ravine
a housewife in silence
holds her dark-haired daughter by the hand
amid the flowers of the field
when freckled with blood
who should turn up
but the jolly butcher
with his droves of lambs.

The Rail

From one end
of the otherwise bare
steel rail in the window
of the village butcher's
hangs an oxtail
from the other
a tongue
all that can be heard
on the empty street
above the sound of the distant sea
endlessly advancing or retreating
the drone of a solitary bee.

Des formes: Forms

Forms come undone
in one great agony
blood leaks
from the slain beast
some congeals within
but names are transcribed
onto the squat pillars.
On certain days
when the villages and alluring cities
are lit up
a face appears
lording it over a body of youths
parading at the foot of ancient battlements.

Ritual

An armoured car drives
wire-meshed visor
paint-bombed
through the barricade
by night a helicopter
circles overhead
in the haze of its noise
men appear in dark back yards
to stare upwards hoping for its light
to come for them
and blind them
that they might curse it.

Police: Police

From a police station overlooking a garden
beside a ditch
and a greenhouse
the turn in the road appears
festooned in gloomy hemlock
a bird lingers
a flower droops
and the long shift goes on
with rule and compass
and coloured ink
day and night striving
to demarcate the world.

Eyebright

Returning from the limits of his world
where a dog barks
by a stream
this side of the unknown
he draws a map of all
he has surveyed that day
giving places their names
in coloured ink,
on his desk a blue flower
whose name he does not know
plucked from the hedgerow
of a road
crossed in the blink of an eye
by a common hare
never to be seen again,
and thus remembered.

Empire: Empire

A mannequin engrossed in shadow
on the ground an iron nail
the blank stare of an emperor
among the leaves
beside the rustic cottages
glimmerings of light cling to a workman's overalls
to the skirts of a woman dreaming
the stairwell is without a handrail
in the alleyway.
The drop-leaf of the escritoire is all blots
beyond the tumult
the sun already well up in the sky.

History

At a school desk
where names are
carved into names
until indecipherable
a boy transcribed
the names and dates
of kings and queens
into his copy-book;
the book is history
its royal blue moiré
dog-eared cover
shimmers
in the empire of the memory
if not forever then
until death.

Les siècles: The Centuries

Looking at the mark
left by the hoof of his thoroughbred
in whose contoured cast
insects were already busy at their needlepoint
the horseman foresaw the invention of printing
then asking for directions
approached a carpenter
who reposing by a rose bush
had taken time out
to contemplate the valley
and would never read a book.

Progress of the Ant

He remembers
sunlit days
when he would lie buried in a book
under a tree thinking
of all the books he had yet
to open
but these days
he thinks of all the books
he will not read before he dies.
An ant zigzags across
a flag of the garden path
carrying a leaf
into what remains of the future.

Mémorable: Memorable

Having drawn water
trembling from the well
with a companion
whose charm had faded
over the years
he sat on the stone rim
to look no further
than an old animal
the colour of the pupils of its eyes
often abused by him
but not so as to die of it.
This is a day when History
appears memorable;
the considerable tree
has writhed from time to time
like a human figure.

Still

He goes
to stand at his door
to gaze at the tree as oft
through time as when it snowed
it bore a ghost of
branches white on black
a stillness
nothing like the thing
that thrashes at his windows
nights he remembers
howling in the wind
he hopes will have died
tomorrow
when he is still about
to stand at his door
to see the tree again,
not to speak of the future.

L'épingle: The Pin

Face to the tide the city looms
over the offing where
the flukes of a troop of whales
beat together beneath the clouds
in spite of all one can hear
the pin that drops
off a chimney mantel
on to a blade of parquet floor
no one has waxed for years.

The Alibi

As to what else
went on within the room
or in the dark beyond
the man remembers pin
after pin dropped
from the woman's
shock of hair
a siren
wailing louder still the more
it neared until
it dwindled into nothing for
he is the man
who when he says he is not
one can hear
a pin drop.

Appel champêtre: Call of the Countryside

Snacking on a piece of bread
smeared with muddy jam
a boy sits on a wall of gleaming clay
his dangling feet shod
with hobnailed boots;
until someone calls him from afar
as yet he does not answer
the same voice
now more insistently calling out
the unique brief syllable of his name
barely troubling the calm of the islands.

The Location Tape

Through the speaker
one can hear
from up on the mountain
the sounds of the city
emanate mutedly
the swash of a car
on the road below
a subdued roar
overlaid with rumble
whether from wind
tape or quarry
the clink of a pebble
a solitary bird cry
twice through what
there was before
vanishing
into the future.

Visages: Faces

Faces which disappoint
our expectations or indeed fulfil them
if one of them turns
the better one sees the curve
of a shoulder gleam.
Somewhere in Colorado
a man draws a bead on
a glint of Venus.
Nevertheless Ney, Marshal of France,
in his Paris prison
plays a plaintive flute.
His forename is Michel
the archangel his patron.
Come evening a woman
covers a few cinders
with their ashes.

Celestial

By day
roof collapsed
onto the floor
of the bombed library
shelves still standing
a man on a ladder
buries his face
open to the sky
in a book.
By night the siren wails
by dawn sounds
the all clear
constellations fade above
the evacuated observatory.

L'oeuf: The Egg

The old lady wipes an egg
with her everyday apron
a heavy ivory-coloured egg
an irreproachable egg
then looks at autumn
through her little dormer window
it makes a fine sight
framed just like a picture
nothing there
is out of season
and the fragile egg
nestled in her palm
is the only thing
still fresh.

Rifle

A man
places an egg
on the stone wall
fifty paces off
a boy
spread flat with his first gun
shuts one eye
draws a bead,
squeezes,
his other eye
jolted open
to see nothing
where once there
was something.

Poursuite: Pursuit

Rust eats right
into the spear head
horses dwell in silence
though the hunt is on
for this man
who runs alone through
labyrinths and ruins
for he never could
reconcile himself to these times.

Missing

Mushroom after seeming
mushroom leads the seeker ever
deeper than he has
been into the woods
two days gone
sounds of helicopter, dog, jeep,
by night thronged
with searchlights
shouts and horns
as for the difference
between mushroom
and toadstool
what would life be
without uncertainty.

Visionnaire: Visionary

The bones of the head throb
the village of an evening
swimming in alcohol
the monstrance
scintillating in the church
when a being enters into trance
in a kitchen piled high
with earthenware and pewterware
and meat and bread
in the surrounding farmlands
each ear of wheat is gorged with night
and the rats in the granaries
tremble with fear in the fullness of life.

According to Scripture

The granaries are filled with black wheat
the rain-barrels frozen solid
but the saviour shall come
to be honoured
among the beasts of the field
among hyenas and ostriches
among the dragons and the owls
he shall be honoured
because he gave water in the desert
and floods in the wilderness
a company of pale millers
marches on the village
where the menfolk neuter sows.

La belle journée: The Beautiful Day

Insects and fishes
steal from shadow to light
fruit still clings to the trees
skimmed by the elegant wing
of a flamboyant bird
then of a drab one.
The blind man scarcely thinks
of his vanished eyes
in the wine-red flower garden.
Out of the blue
the sun bursts into the salon to illuminate
a large painting featuring
an alarming outbreak of rioters.

Revolution

Amid the noise of gunfire
only the blind man
hears his cane
as he taps his way
through streets thronged with rioters
to the printing press
where they cast bullets
from type.

Tragique du temps: Tragedy of the Times

However strong the prison door
the wind blows through below
even as in days of yore
a pale sun sometimes flickers on the creases
of an executioner's jerkin.
In a seaside town
music strikes up
and laying aside his hoe
a labourer sits down to contemplate
the amicable bandsmen
destined for massacre
within the year
declaring their belief in the soul eternal
and the resurrected body.

Interlude

He switched on
the radio to silence
followed by applause
and realized
the music was over
now he remembers
in a far-off battle
shells exploding round him
followed by the rumble
of the orchestra of guns that fired them
the speed of sound ago.

Naturel: What's Natural

The eye lights on things in nature
a dog with random dappled patches
passes by a blade of grass
whistles in the wind
fear descends upon
the narrow walkway
swarming with ants going to work
on the giant ferns.
Indefatigable dazzling
terrestrial strangeness.

In the Woods

Stumbling through
thickets of birdsong
a shrill alarm
incessantly repeated
clear metallic scream
some unknown
hoarser bird rending the air
as if with a word
through the loud rippling rustle
the wind roar swift steady
over everything he
should have been
home by now
might be asleep
behind shuttered windows
no words for how he got
from where to where.

Viande noire: Black Meat

Around precious stones
which grind nothing but
their own dust
the eaters cut into
their black meat
the trees on the horizon
are contoured
like a monumental sentence
images are transfigured
as light leaks away piecemeal
there is a noise of venison
being chewed.
In each and every thing
deepness fattens.

The Hunters

A mile beyond the great bay
window two wives
holding glasses of wine
stare out from into the dark
mist rises from the lake
amid the forest
two husbands who have lost
their quarry
let off their guns at
one and the same time
out on the estuary
two ships sound their foghorns
in and out of sync
then vanish.

La mer et la terre: Sea and Land

Above a sea gone calm
in the fissures of a reef grow
flowers, a wounded
curlew limps
lost in the back lane is the sound of claws
a meadow goes brown
someone says to the young one 'sit straight'
brightness fades
from a sky
that yields no star nor ray of light.

Interval

In the living quarters of a lighthouse
perched on a cliff
the keeper peruses an old magazine
filled with gloomy photographs
to save himself
from falling asleep
to the sound of the waves
vast tracts of silence spread everywhere
the fires of war smouldering
beside the sleeping gazelles.
On land or at sea men still
count the seconds
between blinks of light.

Hors durée: Out of Term

Safe and sound the fishes
are forgotten
in the gloomy pond
veiled by shades
dogs watch on being
witnesses of man;
the groaning of the hollow oak
the cry of a distant bird
strike the ear of the horseman returning
from a thirty years' war.

Echo

Where the house was
shards
of blue willow pattern
are heard
underfoot
overhead
a bird sings from
an unknown bough
and over
someone else's house
a helicopter hovers
as it did an age
ago over
this one overwhelming
it with noise.

Sans connaître l'heure: Knowing Not the Hour

Prisoners of war
sing as one
in a no-man's-land
knowing not the hour.
Gardens dug by moonlight
from the wasteland
stretch meagrely into the distance
sexless ephemeral flies
swarm round the lamps
in houses of clay
little lizards make their dwellings
stretched out on their black ceilings.

The Star

Still not a day goes by but something
is turned up
whether by plough or by stumble
shell-casings, shrapnel, belt-buckles;
over the moss of a pond
formed in a crater mayflies dance in a haze
of their own twilight
until vanishing
in the dark
a little lizard climbs towards the star
he sees from
the hole in a soldier's helmet.

Dire d'un soldat: A Soldier's Statement

My brow my eyes my nose
my mouth which speaks to you
seem not made for this war
says the soldier
the world keeps on turning
to the spattering of young blood
I see the foliage shudder
the road bending in on itself
the looming ruin no one visits.

Bed

Framed by grey steel
his blanket is a regulation grey
freckles of coarse oatmeal
flecks of madder in it
a moth beats against
the glass chimney
of a lamp
near to expiry
from afar he hears
the groans of the tree that beats
against the last window standing
in the moribund asylum.

Muraille: Yard Wall

As a purplish rubble stone
ill fitted to the mortar
and split by frost
will nevertheless hold everything together
so the simple man
who every dawn
turns the key in the lock
takes a turn around the flowerbed
throws a bone to the black dog
will die alone pinned to his wall
seeing columns of smoke rise
from the fugitive horizons.

Trompe l'oeil

Everything held together
by wire, braid, buttons, nails
a woman's calling card
a snapshot of a soldier
a scrap of grey blanket
pinned to the board
an airmail envelope
a still blank blue
the sky through a window
that when everything
else is collapsing
opens.

La bête: The Beast

Seated in the body of a lodge
approached by ancient roads
lives a beast
who shuns the world
rooms lead into rooms
doors close by themselves
and the nights draw in
perfumed by a thorn tree.
All beasts of his kind
dwell in him.

Earshot

Banners held aloft
against a prevailing wind
swords glinting in
an intermittent sun
they do what must be done
as has been done
since when
they had begun to walk
these roads endlessly
ending in cul-de-sac
out of earshot
behind fife and drum
a blackbird improvises on
the obbligato
to its territory.

Pensées d'octobre: October Thoughts

How good it is
to drink this fine wine
all by oneself
when evening illuminates the coppery hills
no hunter any longer sets his sights
on the lowland game
our friends' sisters
look lovelier than ever
regardless of the threat of war
an insect stops
then starts again.

Throwback

Children throwing stones
and bottles over the brick wall
topped with broken bottles
ruby amber green
need not know who
drank the wine
all those years ago
nor what lies on the other side
except that it throws back.

Par les champs: Through the Fields

They see these same fields
quickset with hedges every day
in an approximation of time
they weigh on an enormous pair of cracked scales
powerless to comprehend
how many ears of wheat
are stirred by a breeze
women display themselves by lamplight
a high blank wall grows ever longer
sometimes there
intervenes
a fleeting kiss upon the lips.

Time

The scales of Justice atop
the courthouse pediment
are drilled with holes
lest rainwater
disturb the equilibrium
the heavens open
an inmate is set free
a sentence done
to walk the dark
mile into the city
a nightwalker stands by
an aperture from which
intervenes
the mouth of a gun.

Les livres et l'amour: Books and Love

The books that throng the bedchamber
are set atremble like aeolian harps
when the wind blows from the orange groves
and the letter embedded in the page
adheres to
the white linen paper
and the war thunders from afar
into the blaze of autumn
killing both mistress and lover
on the border of an ancient shoreline.

The Wall

A breeze riffles
the pages of a book left open
at an open window
a man gazes out across
the roofs to where his quarter
of the city borders
on another
then down storey
after storey to
the back yard
wall of crumbling brick
the sickly ivy has yet to climb
to its skyline
of green glass shards.
Again he shuts the window to write
in the book with no end in sight.

Part Three

Sans courage: Without Courage

New courage is needed
for him who returns home
but there is only time, space
the tail end of a periwinkle blue sky
climbing the stairs
he hears a murmuring repeating
God is dead
man too
he stops, the silence dazzles
he composes a face
to take him on up to the attic rooms
almost empty except for childhood.

Translation

A boy leans out
the attic window
of an empty house
that overlooks
the countryside he dreams
of flying over by the time
he descends
landing after landing from where
he has been, the house
reoccupies itself
its occupants
addressing him
as if he had not been
changed in the meantime
that is elsewhere.

Regards: Gazes

A sick man
gazes for ages
at a drop of water
which reflects
an exquisite landscape
a port-wine stain
shaped like France
dwells on his face.
The foam of a tart cider
fizzles out on the dark table
a pan of milk seethes away
all the time
a little before nightfall
in this corner of the world
where eyes
see a moment a long way off.

Wavelength

To see the city from
above that was once
a web glittering with dew
by night the navigator
aims by the spider silk
cross hairs of his bomb sight
years go by
a Dresden milkmaid
shivers on a marble mantelpiece
responding to the bomb
the speed of sound ago
a surveillance helicopter
spins
in the web of its own noise.

L'arc de triomphe: The Triumphal Arch

The man seated in the stairwell
for long hours
dwells on fateful beauty
the treads and handrail are of oak
worm-holed and waxed over the years.
In the shadows calmed by a frail woman
he seizes her hand.
Were the couple to look out from the skylight
they would see encircled by arid fields
the Roman triumphal arch
today but a lofty remnant,
the colour of burnt bread.

Sanctuary

She leads the wounded man
by the hand by night
through the brickfields to sleep
in a broken kiln
soldiers ransack the city
the couple make their way
through the once lofty chimney-stacks
toppled into
brick upon brick
made from the clay
they rest on.

Marée: Tide

The colours of fish
ebb in the white mornings
from time to time
the vendor's cornet sounds
along with the death knell
dogfish are scrutinized
by affable men
looking for something nice to eat.
Who wants to go back by way
of the roads of yesterday
cries a widow's son
breathing the odour
of all kinds of black kelp
drifting far and wide
across land and sea.

Beach

From the steeple
miles inland
above the harbour silted
beyond living memory
he hears the death bell
linger on its wavelength
washing over shards
of medicine bottles smoothed
milky blue
amid the glistening pebbles
bladderwrack pops underfoot
though he has not yet stirred
from where he has been
a fish gasping out of water.

La porte: The Door

The labourer bends to his hoe
until nightfall
he says that long ago
they'd use a pig's tail
to bolt the cellar door
that's now worn to death,
it groans, he hears it.
What sort of future, he says,
lies in wait for us.
The chained dogs at his feet
fall asleep.

The Shed

Well rusted
the latch on the ill fitting door
with a groan it opens
to spade, scythe and hatchet
untouched since
who knows when so high
have horsetail and hemlock grown
in the garden, a dog barks
in the distance beyond
the shuttered house
getting ever nearer
the earth smells of earthworms.

Par ce jour: In This Light

Through and through
in this broad daylight one sees
the empty bowl upon the table
in the depths a glimmering play of shadows
among the passers-by
someone picks up a pin
under a sky growing darker
the more the lamps are being lighted.
An unruffled body
is fathomed by silence.
Images from memory
will resurface
in the due course of the evening.

Lullaby

As night follows day
a fish sleeps
in the boughs of a tree
a cradle rocks
on a still pond
the dreamer stirs
a pin drops
from the console top
the fish falls
into her lap
from the tree that taps
at her bedroom window
birdsong wakes her
from her sleep.

Signes pour voyageurs: Signs for Travellers

Travellers of the great spaces
when you see a girl
coiling in her resplendent hands
the great black fleece of her hair
and furthermore
when you see
outside a dismal bakery
a horse slumped in death
by these signs you will know
that you are among humankind.

Then Again

Deep in the province
is an ancient lodge
forbidden to the traveller
beside the woodshed
chopping-block a white chicken
nods at the red earth,
pecks at then
picks up a straw
and drops it.
A door creaks open.
Swords and axes
gleam in the vestibule.

Le chant: The Song

From this bare room
where soot-flecks were
turning silvery
a voice came forth
to celebrate a woman's hair
shimmering with glints of blue;
the man singing
in his sleek jacket
and grey flecked shirt
opened the window
on a wild countryside;
a rake gently
caressed a path
in the clear light stilled
by an expectation of birds.

Hereafter

The death bell
but an echo in the memory
from a gravel walk
a rake is heard
erasing the footsteps
to and from the grave.
Perched on the wing
of a funerary angel
a blackbird sings helplessly
carried away
by the sound of its own voice.

Sous le soleil: Under the Sun

A horseman advances
his horse
nostrils steaming
goes from walk to trot
over the blue ore
leaves wither under the march of the clouds
the cataract booms
resounding fallout after fallout
in the fields grey rabbits burrow
under the sun everything appears
a symbol of nothing.

Run

The man rises from the ground
from prone to crawl to creep
and after as long as it takes
to stand, to break into a run
from all that are after him
for what he has not done
in the underworld
below his moving feet
the grey rabbits do
what they have always done.

L'île: The Island

Upon the castle lake
there is an island still
where ageing swans are kept
it serves no other purpose but their rest
no woman hides there any longer
whether out of love or by design
the daisy grows out of the earth
and the slowness that was returns.

Echo Lake

Rooted
by the headlights
of an unmarked car
parked where
the woods give out
hands cupped around
his mouth
his face a megaphone
he stands on the shore
he might be shouting
out into
all that is reflected
in the dark lake
if so nothing answers.

La ruine: The Ruin

In his dream the officer
walks down the line
reviewing the troops
while the clerk
makes a deletion in the roster
with a black metal-edged ruler.
Outside looms the ruin
with a solitary window
in its dilapidated wall.

The Riot

With sledgehammers
they break down the walls
of their back yards
into bricks for missiles.
A mile away
in the office block of the brick factory
every window has been bricked up
save one
by whose light the clerk
draws a line under the final reckoning
with a black metal-edged ruler.

Effacement: Under Cover

The grass has grown even longer
over the deep pit
a man walking keeps an eye on
the long-drawn-out cloud
frayed like his grey homespun;
dogs bark discordantly
at the yawning horizons
for all that this is peace
the light of day submits
once more it will be required
to cut one's bread by night
seated on the rustic chopping-block
with the final reckoning
imponderable death.

What Light There Is

By night
a flotilla of helicopters
circles above a city
never seen but heard
a noise indistinguishable
from that of the world
beyond its waves
from time to time
pierced by
a lightning stroke
the shriek of a night bird.

Au bord de l'océan: At the Ocean's Edge

It is a given that
from time to time
the child in the twilight
hears a sea breeze
rustling thorny plants
a gentle dying mother
tells him a story
on the beach a greyhound
quickens its dainty pace
impressing point after point
upon the pure sand
in the workshop built of floorboards
the indefatigable printer
carefully composes
the future decree.

Night Music

In the burned-down library
a man manipulates a keyboard
searching for a passage in the cloud
that might shed light
on what he has in mind
the constellations glitter overhead
in roofless space
from time to time
the wind kicks a tin can down the street
a roulette trickle
stops and starts
shouts from the crowd
in a floodlit stadium
greyhounds pursue the grey electric being
that eludes them time
and time again.

Le charme: The Spell

By virtue of a charm
a maiden dreams
she slips into the cut diamond of her ring
while the fishes sprung from the water
lie gasping on the spring meadow
illusory world
harboured by the sun concealed or not
without respite on earth
and on the waters.

The Eagle

Water would flow
in runnels to cool an emperor's palace
that now lies in ruins
or was heard to drip
from a tap inexorably wearing away
the stone
or was it the drip
of the candles that night
the chosen few
were seated together for the last time
below the emperor at a table
whose centrepiece was
an eagle made of ice.

Grainetier: Seed Merchant

The day not yet ended
a man sleeps
under a sky without fear
soon he must lug
the maize and the barley
the mousey grey buckwheat
the pinkish bran
then vanish down the lane
humpbacked by the last sack
of pallid oats.

Accumulation

He plucked an ear of wheat
and rubbed it with his palm
and blew away the husk
as if to weigh the grains by hand
then let them fall
a pattering upon the rippling road
which took him
to the moiré cover
of the book of scruples, pennyweights and drams
shimmering the snow
in weightless dropping fractions
adding up
to inches on the mile of yards from school
the schoolboy vanishing
into the dusk
of ounces, pounds and tons.

Paroles: The Given Words

There was talk of alleged love affairs
around the antique table
well versed with worm
the iron warming on the stove
a pot of lentils stewing darkly
through the open doorway
the beauty of the tart foliage
and some birds with red throats
in the face of human words
ruled by a time-tested syntax
took one's breath away.

The Given Name

In a junk shop
from a bookcase
riddled with woodworm
he takes a book
blows the dust from it
opens it
at a coloured plate
to behold
the emerald bird
that dazzled for a moment
on the threshold of the world
outside his door
threescore years ago
whose name he did not know
until now.

Fourmis noires: Black Ants

Hands in his pockets he gazes
at the world of black ants
their lacquer-coloured blood
their stings and spurs
their white larvae
trembling at the reverberations
of a struck bell
the violin of his youth sleeps in a coffer
and the night begins to broadcast its stars
across the celestial chart.

The Saw-player

A bell sounds
the passing hour
an ant falls
into a crack
another is crushed
by a passing foot
the veteran
with no legs
propped against the wall
puts bow to saw
to make it keen
of love and loss.

La musique des sphères: The Music of the Spheres

He was following the frozen road
iron keys clinking in his pocket
thinking of nothing, sole fraying from his boot
he stumbled on the cylinder
of an old tin can
which for a few seconds rolled its cold emptiness
wobbled and came to a halt
under a sky enamelled with stars.

Berceuse

Under a bronze sky
the clocks begin to whirr
the bells resounding noon
one by one some but a ting
among others that clank or boom
ongoing is their music
gonging past the hour
a melancholy car horn parps
a harness clinks
a swing cradle
creaks and swings
a child gurgling at a washing-line
of wind chimes made of old tin cans.

Ombres et lueurs: Shadows and Shimmers

In the shade of the walled garden
a whole world is devouring
everything before it
enter the officer on home leave
in his uniform loaded with black braid
a lobate leaf
quivers in the north wind
holding on to a table top
square as his hand
a man dwells
in the swarm of his own bees
while his wife
crumbles stale bread
in a circle of birds blessed by her gesture.

The Horizon

The sailor on shore leave
staggers out from an inn
where the few of a crew
are singing of war
and onto the beach
of a windswept shore
to find his feet on a sea
of cobbles and pebbles,
rocks, stones he has no name for
washed up by what waves
over the ages from
places he has never been.
Bewildered from the dark
he hears the cries of the few
calling out his name.

Lancinant: Transfixion

The sleeper's head lolls on to his chest
in the acrid afternoon
of dreams that clutch at his heart.
One hears the footfall on the path
of a man in fine shoes
his youth past
never having worked the land
nor served under armies,
he stops to catch his breath
sets off again counting every step
the smoke of the day blurs.
Of a sudden someone in a village
can no longer read or speak.

Transfiguration

The valves of one's heart
open and close
to the pulse of blood
without one's knowing it
one can be betrayed.
Feel, says the man laying the boy's fingers
on his wrist,
God never shuts one door
but He opens another.
A great wind blows
in an upstairs room
on whose floor an old man
writhes and speaks in tongues
of the souls that dwell
in the mind
like tongues of fire.

Choses: Things

Stricken, things oscillate for a long time
before lapsing
into voiceless immobility.
A girl eavesdrops at a threshold
whose unyielding door
has long been wont to groan
and by night, stripped of bodice
breasts shiver in dead silence
while in the woodshed
animals cut across each other
and bleed alone.
Hung on the wall a ceremonial sword
is being
eroded by its own rust.
Each thing works quietly away
clocks stopped a long time ago
at the hour when friends sigh
the more they search for laughter.

Passed Naval Censor

Mooring lights reflected
rigging ticks and chinks above
in the house that looms
above the harbour
a man transcribes
a letter from his dead father
only now come to light.
A great moon hangs above
place name blanked he writes.
Were he to look out the window
he would see the same moon
below the rooftop of the house
reflected in the harbour.

Travaux: Works

Working through the fog
the weaver of tapestries
embroiders on and on.
A brown bowl rests
on the long outline of a table
a red insect is about to board.
Beauty sculpted slowly
composes herself
brought to life by the cold
in a giant studio
looming over the precipice
where flourish immortal plants.

Night Shifts

The watchmaker
magnified in eye scrutinizes
the shimmering hairspring
held in his pinion
beyond the rooftops
lie the high dark woods
under a face of porcelain
the colour of clouds
in the downstairs room
the seamstress is washing her hair
before a mirror
in a tin basin dented like the moon.

N'en peut mais: Out of One's Hands

Solomon had nothing proclaims a worker.
Nowhere will you find a lovelier wee mite
says a woman of her sleeping daughter.
Bombardiers to your guns
howls a brigadier
amid the mud and the mire of a plain
and his son in the thick of it.
Roses yield their perfume
in a walled garden
muddled by the work
of spade iron and slow rake.
It's out of the hands
of this man who is eating
in the middle of a warm day.

Behold

No more beautiful array
the lilies of the field
here today
the next cast into the oven
the turn comes
at the end of a furrow
where a man leans
on the end of a spade
his day's work done
faraway
cloud after cloud blossoms
above the city
leaving what remains to be
shovelled from the street.

Image grise: Grey Image

Frail and powerful moments go on
for whatever time it takes
for the deadwood to be gathered
abruptly they say the time to act is now
believing in the day
when they shall rise from the grave
as on the grey image
thrown to the fire
where it is made to writhe,
a being incinerated.
Others believe
they shall be raised on high inasmuch
as through the world their dust-motes whirl
without tomb or monument.

The Cloud

When the bell tolls
however still it be
the grasses shiver
footsteps echo leading
to and from
where they have been
under all
there is to see
on the blue dome
the wisp above
the crematorium.

Fichu noir: Black Scarf

A kind of rapture
memory never wearies of
suddenly descends upon
those sitting at the table
the lamp smokes.
A broad headscarf comes to sink down
at the feet of the Lord God
depicted in a painting.
Under cover birds perch
and fall silent
the woman whose clothes
will end up in tatters
says as she picks up
the square of black wool
there's no cheating the years
around her face
the proposition founders.

The Fall of the Cards

Light dapples
fall to the ground the hunter covers
under the forest canopy
game on his mind.
Before the gunshot
woodpigeons funnel themselves
upwards
and outwards with the sound
of a thousand cards
being shuffled
remembers
the boy rapt in building
another trembling
floor to the house
that collapses before
his breath
twilight falls.

Les images: Images

A child gently lifted up
a deep dark wine
leaves woven into wreaths
a body shimmering
into sweeter blindness
sometimes ask
for no conclusion
but form in the eye
ephemeral images
remembered yet again
in the twilight
of black heathlands.

Reach

As the blind man
described the sunned spine
of a certain book
nine shelves up
third from the left
on the wall of shelves
that faces the great bay window,
his reader, reaching for it
from atop the library ladder
was brought to think
how much more of the room
the blind man must see
having grown it
in his memory for years.

Brodequin: Laced Boot

Methodically tying
a well worn grey lace
under the greening sign
a man has rediscovered
some appreciation
for the relics of old decency
his eyes have seen
these eyelets
ringed with yellow brass
the meandering wrinkles
in a borrowed boot
whose every nail will mark
the humus of the plain
till the day of his death
so many steps away.

One Day When

The boy bows
to do up his lace
the yellow brass
of the monastery bell
shimmers from afar
under a sky blank
as the spaces between
the feint blue lines
of the pages yet to go
in his school notebook.
A red insect trembles
from the green moss
between two flagstones
then begins to creep
towards
the unimaginable horizon.

Notes

PAGE 21

'Out' is based on a passage in John Clare's autobiography, where he goes out one morning to gather rotten sticks from the wood, then has a feeling that he wants to wander about in the fields. He gazes over the yellow furze of Emmonsales Heath stretching into the distance, and imagines 'that the world's end was at the edge of the horizon and that a day's journey was able to find it'. The young Clare begins to walk, losing not only all sense of direction but that of time; he finds himself in another world but, as night begins to fall, chance puts him on the right track home, where he finds his parents in great distress and half the village out hunting for him. Jean Follain, for all his mistrust of the English language, was an admirer of Clare's poetry. In a letter written to *Nouveau Commerce* in 1965 Follain praises Clare's transparency, the near absence of metaphor in a poetry where all things are equal in the field of vision, words touching things directly, as in Follain's own poetry.

PAGE 23

'In Memory' is indebted to Seamus Heaney's 'Personal Helicon'.

PAGE 95

'The Location Tape' is based on a soundscape of recordings made by Úna Monaghan for *Owenvarragh*: A Belfast Circus on *The Star Factory*, devised according to instructions by John Cage.

PAGES 101 & 109

'Missing' and 'In the Woods' are based on passages from John Cage, *X: Writings '79–'82*.

PAGE 121

'Trompe l'oeil' is based on a passage from T. J. Clark, *Picasso and Truth*.

PAGE 151

'Echo Lake' is based on a painting of the same title by Peter Doig.

PAGE 173

'Passed Naval Censor' is for Carlo Gébler.

PAGE 175

'Night Shifts' is for David Williams,
watchmaker and flute player.

Acknowledgements

Grateful acknowledgement is due to the Estate of Jean Follain. Translations of poems from *Usage du temps* (1943), *Exister* (1947), *Des heures* (1960), *Appareil de la terre* (1964), *D'après tout* (1967) and *Espaces d'instants* (1971) appear by kind permission of Gallimard. Poems from *Territoires* (1953) appear by kind permission of Host Publications. Poems from *Présent jour* (1978) and *Ordre terrestre* (1986) appear by kind permission of Éditions Fata Morgana.

Some of these poems have previously appeared in *The Edinburgh Review*, *Icarus*, *The Lifeboat*, *Poetry London*, *Poetry Proper*, and *Trinity Journal of Literary Translation*.

'*Soulier renoué*: Shoelace Tied' and 'Out' were first published in an essay in *The Open Field: The John Clare Series* (Naughton Gallery at Queen's, Belfast, 2013), a catalogue accompanying an exhibition of paintings by Clement McAleer based on John Clare's *Journey Out of Essex*. I am grateful to the artist for my conversations with him about the project, which led me to re-examine Clare's work, and subsequently affected some of the writing in this present book.

My translations of the poems of Jean Follain would no doubt have turned out differently had I not consulted translations by Kurt Heinzelmann, Heather McHugh, W. S. Merwin, and Christopher Middleton. I am indebted to them for their various interpretations, which guided mine to a greater or lesser degree. I am grateful to Tess Gallagher, Paul Nolan, and Alan Gillis who read much of the work in progress.